Unusual Pets

Written by Chris Madsen
Illustrated by Julie Cooke

© 1992 Henderson Publishing Limited

Henderson
Woodbridge, England *Publishing*

CHOOSING A PET

Cuddly pets
Some animals love to be stroked and cuddled. This is because they like touching one another, as we do. Some animals hate it, though. If you want a pet to cuddle, make sure you choose one that enjoys being touched, or both of you will be disappointed.

Interesting pets
Imagine being able to jump out of your own skin! Some pets can do just that, and if you keep one you can watch it happen. Unusual pets do other unusual things, too. If you choose a really different kind of pet, you could even discover something about it that nobody ever knew before.

KNOW YOUR PET

Make sure you have time

When you have a pet, you are its best friend. It depends on you for all its needs - food, water, shelter, even air. A wild, free animal can go and hunt for food when it feels hungry, or move into the shade when it gets too hot, but a pet only gets what you give it and has to stay where you put it. Keeping a pet takes time and trouble, every day. You can't say 'sorry' to a pet.

Easy-to-keep pets

If you don't have a lot of time to spend caring for a pet, it doesn't mean you can't have one. Just choose an easy-care pet. Spiders don't need to be fed every day, and snails can last a long time if you go away on holiday.

Suit your pocket

Some pet shop pets are expensive to buy. They may need expensive cages and food, too. Before you get a pet shop pet, make sure you know exactly how much it will cost to keep, and that you can afford it. If you aren't rich, this doesn't mean you can't have a pet. Wild temporary pets can cost almost nothing to keep. This doesn't mean they are worthless, though - always remember that every single animal's life is precious.

Who owns animals?

Animals aren't toys. They belong to themselves, not to people. We must look after our pets as we would look after our guests, for that is what they are.

MAKING A TERRARIUM

What is a terrarium?

A terrarium is a small piece of the world you can watch without getting your knees dirty or a crick in the neck. Almost anything can go into it - snakes, spiders, caterpillars, crickets, snails and other small wild invertebrates you may find and want to keep for a while.

A small piece of the world

A terrarium is like an aquarium. But instead of filling it with water to make a tiny pond, we put soil and plants into it to make a little bit of the dry-land world.

What to use

It is best to use a real aquarium tank, but a big glass jar would do nearly as well. If you want to see your pets, the sides must be transparent. It doesn't matter to them - they don't care whether they can see you or not.

How to begin

First, spread a layer of soil on the bottom. Plant grass and a few larger plants in the soil, and put some stones or gravel on top of the soil between the plants. A piece of rotten wood will give shy pets somewhere to hide away, and a twig or two will make a climbing-frame.

Put a lid on it

A terrarium must have a top to keep your pets inside, or they will soon be wandering about the house.

Air

The top must have plenty of air-holes. The size of the holes depends on what animals you want to keep. If you want to keep ants, the holes will have to be much smaller than if you want to keep crickets! Try to make a hard top from fine wire mesh. If this isn't possible, a bit of net curtain will do quite well; use elastic to keep it on, though, because many creatures are a lot stronger than they look.

Food

Another thing to think about is how you are going to feed your pets. Make the top so that you can put in food (and new pets) without allowing the animals already in there to escape. You will also have to take food out if it goes mouldy. The easiest way to arrange this is to open a paper-clip to make a double-ended hook and hang the food on this.

Water

Don't forget to water your terrarium. Outside, it sometimes rains. Make rain for your terrarium sometimes. Remember the soil is only shallow - don't drown your pets!

TERRAPINS

What are terrapins?
Terrapins are reptiles. These small relations of turtles are no ordinary pets; they are very special and exotic, so they need very special care and a lot of love.

Where to get them
Terrapins are pet shop animals. Choose one that makes swimming movements when you hold it out of the water.

What to keep them in?
You will need an aquarium tank with a thermostatic water heater plus an overhead lamp. For one terrapin, it should be at least 12" x 12" x 15". Three terrapins will need about three times this space.

The tank should be filled with water to a depth of twice the length of your terrapins (head-to-tail, not shell length), and there must be a smooth rock for them to climb on to bask in the heat of the lamp. Everything must be perfectly clean at all times.

What temperature?
The water should be heated to somewhere between 29°C and 34°C. Lower may make them hibernate, and higher could kill them. The lamp should have a 60-watt bulb. It will need to be switched on each morning and left on for at least 8 hours. Terrapins like to sleep in the dark, so don't leave the light on all the time.

When to feed?

Terrapins like to eat once a day. The best time is in the early evening, just before the light goes off.

Where to feed?

It is best to take your terrapins out to feed them in a special bowl. They need water to feed in, but putting food into their home tank will pollute the water. The feeding water should be as warm as the water in the home tank, because cold water will make them sulky and they won't eat.

What to Feed?

The best basic diet is the sort of food that pet shops sell specially for turtles. To this, you should add some chopped lettuce and a little fruit, plus a little minced liver (or earthworms) and fish (canned sardines or tuna with the oil or sauce washed off will be fine). They don't need to have all of this every day - just like you, they prefer a variety of food.
NEVER FEED FAT TO A TERRAPIN.

Shell food

Terrapins cannot make a shell from nothing. The best way to help them grow a strong, hard shell is to sprinkle a little ground-up cuttlebone on their food each day.

FIRST CATCH YOUR PET

What is a pooter?
It's not a good idea to start off by squashing your new pet. Using a pooter means you don't have to touch them at all, so there is no danger of hurting them - or of them hurting you!

How to make a pooter
You will need:
a pot with a lid, two different coloured bendy drinking straws, some Band-aid, a scrap of muslin or net curtain, and small rubber bands or thread.

First, the most difficult bit is to make 2 holes in the lid to push the straws through. They should fit tightly, but you can use Band-aid to fix them if the holes are too large. Push one straw in deep. Fix the muslin or net over the end of the other straw before you push it in. Put the top on the pot, and there is your pooter.

Try it out
Practise on a grain of rice. Point the deep straw at the rice grain and suck sharply through the straw with the net on it. Hopefully, the rice will end up in the pot. If your pooter works, now try it out on real animals.

Warning: Remember which colour is the suck-through straw. NEVER suck through the wrong straw - if the pot is empty, your target will land up against the net. If you already have something in the pot, it will go into your mouth!

Catching bigger things

Slow-moving pets are easy to catch. But to catch a fast-moving one, you have to be sneaky. One way is to pop a jar over the top and then slide a stiff card or thin piece of plastic underneath. This works well for beetles on the ground.

Collecting tree creatures

The best way to do this is to shake a branch. Spread a sheet underneath and use a stick to bang or shake the branch. You can then poot up what lands on the sheet. Some things might land on your head...so WEAR A HAT!

KEEPING CATERPILLARS

What are caterpillars?

A caterpillar is a baby moth or butterfly. We call it a larva. When it has finished growing, it will stop eating and turn into a pupa (chrysalis). Inside the hard pupa shell, the caterpillar's fat, soft body will change into a grown-up insect. If you care for your caterpillars well, you can see all this happen, before your very eyes.

Keeping caterpillars happy

Caterpillars are easy to keep happy. All they want from life is plenty of food and air. Just pop the caterpillars in your terrarium and keep them supplied with fresh leaves to eat every day. If you have no terrarium, a big jar will do. Tree caterpillars will be happy on a leafy twig in a jar of water, as long as there are plenty of fresh leaves to eat.

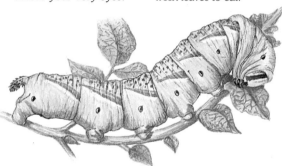

What do caterpillars eat?

Most caterpillars eat leaves. Each kind of caterpillar eats a different kind of leaf. When you catch one to keep, be sure to see what kind of leaf it was eating so that you can feed it the same leaves.

What next?

When your caterpillars have finished growing, they will start to roam around looking for a safe place to pupate. Some like to dig into the ground; others like to hang up on a twig. Each has its own special trick.

Be patient

Now you must leave them in peace. Look at them often, but don't touch. If they are underground, don't keep digging them up to see what's happening! Keep winter pupae in a cool frost-free place. Keep summer ones out of direct sunlight.

The big surprise

Before a moth can fly, it must spread out the wings that grew, all squashed up, inside that cramped chrysalis. This is the best bit of all, and what you have been waiting for. All the help an underground pupa needs is a twig to crawl up; one that is already on a twig needs no help at all. Don't disturb it, just watch.

Time to let go

When the butterfly or moth is ready, it will want to fly away. Let it go, and there will soon be more caterpillars for you to find and rear.

Eggs

If you find eggs like this on a leaf, pick the leafy twig and see what happens, right from the beginning.

Spring or fall?

Spring caterpillars often become adult insects in the same year. Later ones usually wait through the winter before emerging.

SNAILS AS PETS

EASY-CARE PET

Why keep snails?
Snails make perfect pets. They are easy to catch, easy to feed, and get on well with all the other pets in your terrarium. They aren't smelly or noisy, either, and won't upset the neighbours.

What do snails eat?
Land snails eat plants. Most of them will be quite happy with lettuce or other soft leaves. Some snails - the kind that you find under rotten wood - prefer mouldy leaves. Snails cannot bite. They use a tongue like a file to scrape away at their food. If you let a large snail walk across your fingers, you can feel its file tickling your skin as it goes - it isn't nearly strong enough to damage your skin or hurt you.

How do snails move?
Watch a snail travelling on the glass wall of your terrarium, and see the ripples as it glides along on its one big flat foot. It glides on a layer of sticky slime (mucus) that works like glue to stop the snail falling off.

How do snails breed?
To see snails mate, all you need is two of them. Every snail is male and female at the same time. When they mate, they exchange eggs and sperms, then both of them go away to lay fertilised eggs. Some snails have really incredible ways of getting together! If you keep pet snails, you'll have the chance to see what they do.

Recognising snail eggs

Snail eggs look like a cluster of white pearls. They are usually laid in moist soil. If you are very careful, you may be able to put a clump of snail eggs into your terrarium and see them hatch.

Don't be surprised if they hatch into slugs, though, because slugs are just snails without shells and their eggs look the same.

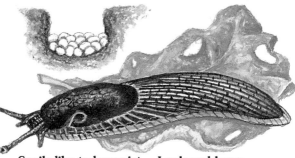

Snails like to be moist

In dry weather snails shut themselves up in their shell and wait for it to rain. Pet snails will do this if you forget to water them. They will come to no harm, but dry snails doing nothing make boring pets!

Look and learn

Watch your pet snail as it goes around doing what snails do. The long pair of tentacles on its head have a black dot - an eye - at the end. It doesn't see much, but it can see light and dark. The short tentacles are for touching and tasting. See how your snail explores its world.

KEEPING SPIDERS

EASY-CARE PET

Catch your spider
There are 65,000 different species of spiders in the world. The one you want is a house spider, the big sort that falls into the bath. You want a female, though, so find her in her web. Once you have her, you can transfer her to her new home in your terrarium or a big jar.

Make her cosy
Spiders don't need much help. They like to build a web in a corner (ask your mother!), so try to arrange your spider's home so that she has a corner to live in. Keep the jar out of the sun, and wait until she has made a web.

Spider webs
Your spider will make a big, untidy tangle of web, but if you look closely you will see that there is a neat tunnel in it. This is where your spider will live while she waits for food to arrive.

Feeding your spider
Web spiders have terrible eyesight; they can't see a fly, and only know it is there by feeling the web vibrate when the fly struggles. So you must give your spider live flies to eat. She won't need many though, about one a week will do.

When you have caught a fly, just pop it into the spider's home jar and wait. Sooner or later, it will blunder into the web and then you can watch your spider go to work.

Male and female

Male spiders are most often seen running about the house looking for a mate. A male spider has two large lumpy feelers by its mouth; a female - the sort you will have chosen for a pet - has thin ones.

Spider courtship

If you put a male and a female together, don't expect them to have a cuddle. A male spider has to be very careful how he approaches a female in her web. She can't see him, so he plucks at the web to tell her he isn't a fly. If it isn't mating time, the female will probably just eat him. If she feels like mating, then she will wait until afterwards before she eats him.

In the wild, the male would have a chance to escape, but in your jar he is doomed!

Spiders eggs

Spiders make a silk cocoon for their eggs. Mother spiders usually guard their eggs until they hatch. If you find an egg cocoon, you can watch the tiny spiders hatch. See how small they are, then try to work out what they could possibly manage to eat!

Why don't spiders stick to their own webs? Spiders don't make all the strands sticky. They run on the dry ones, but a fly can't tell the difference.

KEEPING SILKWORMS

What are silkworms?
Silkworms are tropical moth caterpillars. They spin their silk cocoon to pupate in.

Where to get silkworms
You must go to a pet shop to buy your silkworms. Ask the people there for advice, because the more you can find out, the more successful you will be.

Where to keep them
The best arrangement is a plastic tube with a firm base and a top with holes in. Put a narrow necked container inside, to hold water for a leafy twig.

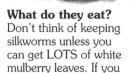

What do they eat?
Don't think of keeping silkworms unless you can get LOTS of white mulberry leaves. If you start with small caterpillars, you can put them straight onto a leafy mulberry twig. Use a soft paintbrush so you don't hurt them. As the leaves are eaten or wither, add a new twig. Wait until most of your silkworms have moved to the new leaves. You can move stragglers over with the paintbrush.

Starting with eggs
Put the eggs into a closed plastic box (no air-holes needed), along with some moist paper tissue but not right on it. When the eggs hatch, do nothing until the caterpillars begin to wander about. Then add a few tender leaves and put the lid on again. Keep them clean: lay fresh tissue regularly on the bottom and don't allow mould to grow on the droppings.

Growing bigger

When the silkworms are big enough, they can be moved to their new home. Put the leaves with caterpillars on among a spray of fresh leaves, and move stragglers with a paintbrush.

Warmth

These are tropical moths and like to be warm, but not too hot. They need plenty of moisture in the air. If their home is water-proof, the leaves will keep the air inside moist.

When they pupate

When your silkworms are fully grown they will start to spin their silk cocoons. After they have finished, put them in a cool place. If you want their silk, wait for two weeks before gently unwinding it. Remember that this will kill the developing moth.

See moths emerge

Leave the pupae alone until they are ready. The adult moths need no food, because they don't eat. They ate all they needed as cater-pillars, and the moths do nothing except mate and lay eggs. If you want your moths to do this, you must give them a bigger cage. This is easy: just replace the lid with a large muslin bag on a wire frame. The moths mate at night, and the eggs will be laid on the muslin. Then you can start all over again, or give some eggs to your friends for them to try.

AN ANTS' NEST

What are ants?
Ants are insects related to bees and wasps. They live in large cities that they build and organise with incredible skill.

Male and female
Most ants have no wings; these are females. Males are the ones with wings that suddenly appear, once a year, in a great swarm.

The Workers
Females do all the work. One female, the Queen ants, lays all the eggs. She is much bigger than the others and doesn't go out. The rest of the females are hunters, soldiers, cleaners and nannies. All that the males do is mate, when the time comes.

Catch your queen
This is the chancy part. It depends on finding a young queen ant, ready to start building her nest. When the winged males are swarming, there will be young winged queens about, too. They fly up, high and the males fly after them to try to catch one to mate with. After mating, the queens come down and shed their wings before looking for somewhere to set up house. This is about the only time you can catch one.

How to begin
All that the queen ant needs is a box of soil, not too wet, not too dry. A terrarium half filled with soil is perfect, but any deep waterproof container will do. If you want to watch what goes on underground, it will need to be transparent. Make the soil look natural by scattering leaves and little twigs about and leave the queen to get on with her job. She won't need to eat anything yet.

The colony grows

The queen will rear her first eggs alone. When the first workers emerge, they will start to look after her and make the nest bigger. Now they will need food.

What to feed ants

You can begin to feed your ants bread and honey, with an occasional scrap of minced meat. Then try all kinds of things and see which they prefer. Choosing food is no problem. The real problem is how to get the food in and out without letting the ants escape! You will have to be ingenious - choose a time when they aren't out and about. Don't let old food stay around to go bad; use a small container you can quickly and easily put in and take out, like a bent soup spoon.

Look and learn

Watch your ants' nest grow, and study your ants to find out how they run their organisation. See the workers gathering food; see the queen laying her eggs and watch the nannies carry them away to rear. If you put a wild ant in there, you may even see the soldiers come out to do battle!

Water

The soil needs to be kept very slightly moist, just as it would be outdoors. Give the nest a fine mist spray occasionally. If grass grows on top of the soil, let it happen.

BUSH-CRICKETS AS GUESTS

What are crickets ?
Crickets and katydids are big insects related to grasshoppers and roaches. There are many different kinds; a few are easy to keep, but most are almost impossible to keep happy for more than a few days.

Catch your crickets
The best time to catch a cricket is when they are chirruping on a warm night. Only the males do this; females are silent. In spite of their noisy habits they are extremely hard to spot...and they are even more difficult to catch! Some kinds try to escape by leaping high, others drop like a stone to the ground. Be cunning, but be careful, because those long legs are easily broken. Have patience, and you will be well rewarded.

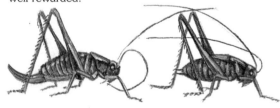

Male and female
It is very easy to see whether you have a male or a female. Females have a long, curved 'horn' at the end of their body, which they use to push their eggs deep into a safe crevice. Males have two little pointed horns there. If you catch a male, you can listen to his cheerful song.

The hotel

Make your cricket comfortable by giving him plenty of furniture. He will want some twigs to climb, some grass, some soil, and perhaps a few stones. A well-stocked terrarium will provide perfect accommodation.

Temporary guests

Wild crickets are definitely only weekend guests. Their way of life is much too complicated for us to be able to offer them more than a hotel room for a few nights. Enjoy them while you have them, but don't make them stay too long or they will surely die.

Feeding

While your guest is in residence, offer him a varied menu. Some crickets eat soft plants, fruit, bread, and other vegetable food; some only eat meat; others eat a bit of everything.

Look and learn

Use the paper-clip method to offer food to your cricket. See what he chooses to eat. He may eat nothing at all; in this case, he should be set free after 24 hours. If he seems to be enjoying your hospitality, you may keep him for a little longer without harming him.

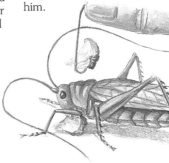

EXTRA-SPECIAL PETS

House crickets

These are quite different from katydids. They live much more happily in captivity. They are more difficult to get, though. If you can obtain some house-crickets, be sure to keep them in a warm place and have a secure cover on their quarters because they can fly! They like to live among stones rather than juicy greenery. Feed them bread and lettuce, provide leaf-mould or crumpled paper for egg-laying, and you could have chirpy pets for life.

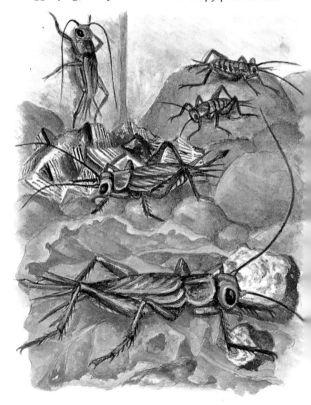

TREE FROGS

What are tree frogs?
Tree frogs are amphibians, like other frogs, but they spend most of their adult life climbing trees. Their toes have little sticky pads for clinging, instead of webs for swimming.

Where to get tree frogs
You must buy your tree frogs from a pet shop. Ask the pet shop owner for advice, because you will need to know as much as possible to make sure your frogs stay healthy and happy.

Accommodation
Tree frogs are busy little beasts and they love to explore. They need a big terrarium, set on end to give them height for climbing.

There must be plenty of moisture, for their delicate skin dries up very easily. Daily misting is essential. Provide branches to climb, with moist greenstuff underneath, and a dish of water.

Feeding
Tree frogs eat live food. Their wicked-looking slit eyes cannot spot food unless it is moving. In the wild, they hunt beetles and flies. If you cannot catch live flies easily, you can buy maggots ('gentles') from fishing-tackle shops or pet shops.

Your tree frogs may eat them as they are, or you may need to wait for the adult flies to develop. An easy way to put a fly in the terrarium is to get it into a blown-up plastic bag first. Then quickly pop the bag inside with the top open (but close the terrarium!) until the fly escapes. Your frog will soon spot the fly, and will show you how it stalks and catches its dinner.

Frog-sitters

If you go away on holiday, you can leave your frog-sitter with a supply of ready-wrapped flies. Even the most squeamish person will find this isn't too awful to do. Another trick is to leave some gentles inside to hatch into flies as time goes by, but you may return to find flies buzzing about everywhere! As long as they are kept moist, though, your frogs can safely be left without food for a few days, BUT MOISTURE IS ESSENTIAL.

Colour changing

When you buy your tree frogs, they will usually be bright green. Don't worry if they turn brown, or even grey, once you get them home. They aren't sick; changing colour is just one of their sneaky little tricks. Watch to see how quickly they can do this. Don't expect them to turn bright red or blue, though - those colours just aren't in their paint box.

Home base

Each tree frog will choose its own special place to live. You will soon be able to find every one of your pets without having to look very hard, no matter what colour they are today.

ODDS AND ENDS

Frog or toad?

The fact is, tree frogs are really toads. Watch how they move their head to look at a fly. Frogs can't do that.

Make your frogs sing

Frogs and toads can hear. When they are ready to mate, they call to one another by puffing up their throat and croaking. Sometimes , you can fool a frog into croaking for you by making a noise he thinks is another frog. Try out different music and see what works.

A COLD-WATER AQUARIUM

A small pond
When setting up your aquarium, aim to make it as much like a real pond as you can. The best water to use is pond-water or rainwater and everything that goes into it should be clean and natural.

How cold?
Cold water doesn't mean you have to put ice cubes in! What it really means is that it ought not to get too warm in Summer. 50-65°F(10-18°C) is fine. An ordinary max-min thermometer will help you to keep the water at the correct temperature.

How to begin
First, you need a watertight aquarium tank. Before you do anything else, decide where it is going to stay and put it there - it doesn't weigh much now, but it will be very heavy when it's full of water! Place your tank on a strong table in a light place, but out of the sun. Now put a sloped layer of washed gravel in the bottom (about 1-2 inches deep), fill up with water, and leave it for a day or two to settle.

The importance of plants

Plants aren't just pretty, they are vital to life. They make oxygen and take away carbon dioxide. Just as trees keep our air good to breathe, water plants give your water pets oxygen to breathe. Choose any pondweed that grows completely underwater. Attach the bottom of each plant to a small stone to help it to grow naturally.

Extra air

If you keep river pets, they might need more oxygen than plants can supply. In a natural river, the moving water gathers air. In your aquarium, you will need to make bubbles with a small air-pump.

Some important rules

NEVER use paint or varnish in the same room as your aquarium. NEVER put copper or brass objects into the water; they are deadly poisons. NEVER use insect or fungus poisons in the same room. That means fly-sprays, plant powders or sprays, and even some wallpaper pastes.

Let nature work for you

You can buy lots of gadgets for aquariums. They can be useful, but remember that natural ponds get by pretty well without help from pet shops. If you stock your indoor pond wisely, nature will take care of itself. Look at a real pond, maybe the one you took the water from. Take some snails, some weed, and some other small creatures from the same pond. Snails will keep the walls clean, and everything else has its own special job, too.

COLD-WATER FISHES

Sticklebacks
There aren't many aquarium fishes that can outshine a male stickleback in his Spring finery. The bright red belly is a sign to other males to keep away. Unless you have a very big tank, don't expect two males to live peacefully together. If you keep a male and a female, and give them lots of weed, you may be lucky enough to see how the male builds his nest, lures the female in to lay her eggs, and then tends them until they hatch. Feed sticklebacks meaty, live food like bloodworms.

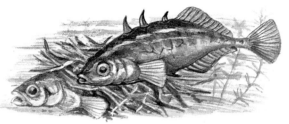

Catfishes
These fascinating fishes make marvellous pets, but beware! They will swallow other fishes up in the twinkling of an eye. They also grow at an incredible rate! Faced with a huge catfish in a small tank, some careless people have been driven to 'liberate' it into a wild pond - with disastrous results, for the catfish has eaten up every other fish there. Think very hard before you decide to buy a dear little catfish! Feed catfishes meaty live food, if you hadn't already guessed it...

Fancy goldfishes

One reason why goldfishes make great pets is because they don't need a lot of oxygen. Another reason, of course, is because they are very pretty. Even an ordinary goldfish is spectacularly coloured, and some fancy kinds are truly impressive.

Celestial. A star-gazing fish with a short tail.
Comet. Has two long streamers on its tail.

Fantail. Has a big, lobed tail like a rippling fan.
Pearlscale. Like a Fantail, but with large bumpy scales.

Veiltail. Has a long, flowing tail.
Moor. Like a black veiltail with huge eyes.
Brambleheads. These have berry-like lumps on their head. Lionheads have a short tail, Orandas have large fins and tail.
Shubunkins. Comet-tailed with an enormous variety of colour patterns.

Caring for goldfishes

Feed on ants' eggs, daphnia, and dried fish-food from the pet shop. Do not overfeed - they don't know when to stop, and will stuff themselves until they die! Left-over food will rot and pollute the water. A sprinkle, once a day (twice in Summer), is enough.

Fishy problems

Aquarium fishes sometimes get diseases. If one of your pets seems 'strange', either in appearance or behaviour, it must be put into a separate tank at once, so that the rest do not catch the disease. After that, you should get expert advice.

RATS AS PETS

TENDER LOVING CARE

Why keep rats?
Rats are very intelligent, naturally clean, and do not smell bad. They are easy to handle, and can even be allowed out of their cage for exercise - your pet rat may even choose to climb on your lap! They are also easy to feed, because they like many of the things we eat. Pet rats are more fun to play with than pet mice.

Choosing your rat
There are many exotic types of rat to choose from. Look for a sleek, glossy coat with no bare patches, a long, perfect tail, bright intelligent eyes and a good bunch of twitching whiskers.

Housing
Like mice, rats gnaw incessantly. They need an all-metal cage with a nest-box off the floor. Hay or wood shavings will make good bedding, and sawdust on the floor will help your pet to keep itself clean. The sawdust will need changing twice a week, bedding less often.

Food and water
Rats drink a lot of water. The best way to give this is with a drip bottle; your inventive pet will soon learn how to use it. Food can be given in a bowl. Base your rat's diet on grain, with some seeds and nuts, and fresh vegetables like carrot and greens. Eggs and milk are good, especially if your pet rat is pregnant.

Entertainment

Rats love to play! They are busy little bodies and will soon get bored in a bare box. A block of wood for gnawing is essential to prevent your pet's teeth from growing too long. A piece of pipe and a ladder will give it something to do. Try out different toys to see what your pet likes.

Handling

A really tame rat can be picked up gently by the scruff of its neck and placed on the palm of your other hand. Alternatively, pick it up securely with both hands. White rats with red eyes are rather short-sighted. Your pet may be very tame, but it might not see you coming and could be shocked enough to nip you if you do not understand its problem, so don't sneak up on it.

Male and female

Male rats are more placid than females. They also get on better together. Two males often become best friends; two females might not. If you'd like to keep a breeding pair, you will need two cages so that the male and female can be kept separately after mating. Once a male has had a mate he will be less friendly with other males. WARNING: Immediately after mating, rats can be very bad-tempered for several hours! When your pet is pregnant, try not to disturb her. The babies will be born in just over 3 weeks.

The bottom line

Never, never try to make a pet of a wild rat. It can't be tamed, and could carry dangerous diseases. Always get your rat from a pet shop or a friend.

STICK-INSECTS

What are stick-insects?

Believe it or not, these are relatives of roaches and grasshoppers, like the crickets.

Why stick-shaped?

When you invite your friends to come and see your stick-insects, the secret becomes clear. Not many people can spot a stick-insect, even when they are told where to look! In the wild, looking like a twig is a very good way to hide, like standing very still in a waxworks museum. This is called camouflage.

Housing

Stick-insects live very well in the same kind of cage you would make for silkworms, or a terrarium on end would do fine. All they really need is a bunch of twigs to hide on and plenty to eat.

Where to get them?

Stick-insects are pet shop animals. Common stick-insects are fairly easy to find, but there are also some with prickles that make even more unusual pets.

Curiouser and curiouser

One of the many peculiar things about stick-insects is that they hardly ever mate. Very few eggs hatch into males, and the females lay fertile eggs perfectly well without ever having met a mate. We don't even know what the males of some species of stick-insects look like - which might be because there aren't any!

Feeding

Common stick-insects thrive on privet leaves - another unusual thing about them, since privet is poisonous to many animals. Simply put a jar of water with some privet twigs into the terrarium. They also eat ivy and holly leaves. Prickly stick-insects are supposed to feed on rose and raspberry leaves, but very little is known about them.

Temperature

The speed of egg-laying, hatching and growth depends entirely on temperature. For example, eggs laid in winter and kept unheated may take 8 months to hatch while eggs in a warm place can hatch in 2 months.

Breeding

When the females are fully-grown (after about six moults, which takes about 6 months), they lay two or three eggs a day, just dropping them as they go around feeding at night. During its life, a female may lay several hundred eggs. Sometimes, an egg hatches into a small, thin stick-insect. This is a male.

Night life

During the day, your stick insects will be really busy pretending to be twigs, so don't expect a circus. At night, they unbend to eat and lay eggs. One advantage of this is that you won't miss a thing while you are at school.

Look and learn

Watch your stick-insects to learn more about their strange ways.

SNAKES

Why keep a snake?

Most people keep snakes for their beauty. Like fishes, they are lovely to look at. Unlike a fish, though, a snake can be handled. Somebody who has never touched a snake will be surprised by the way it feels. Far from being cold and slimy, its skin is warm and dry.

Be prepared

A snake's needs are quite simple, but they are very precise. Keeping one as a pet means learning a great deal about its natural way of life. It won't wag its tail, or purr, or even cry, so the only way you can tell if your snake is happy is to watch it closely to see that it remains glossy and fit.

Choosing a snake

It is very important to buy your snake from a reputable pet shop. There are two reasons for this: firstly, most countries have strict laws to protect wild snakes; secondly, it is the best way to be sure of finding out how to care for your special - and expensive - pet properly. If a pet shop cannot provide lots of information about a snake it has for sale, then it is wise to go away and look elsewhere.

Will it bite?

If a snake couldn't bite, it would starve. Every other pet can bite, too! An important thing to remember is that snakes can't hear, so if you creep up on your pet he may just be surprised enough to snap - but even a mouse will do this.

Critical temperature

The correct temperature is absolutely vital for snakes. This is the most important thing you can provide for your pet. Find out exactly what its favourite temperature is, and then use a heating-lamp and thermometer to make sure the terrarium is kept at that temperature.

Housing

A terrarium makes an ideal home. It should have a dry gravel floor and contain a place to hide, such as a flowerpot laid on its side. A shallow dish of water and one or two large rocks will complete the furniture.

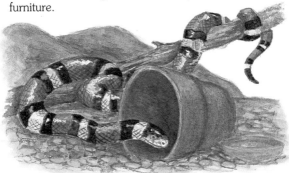

Facing up to feeding

Feeding a snake is not for the faint-hearted. The good news is that snakes don't have to be fed very often; once a week is generally quite enough. The bad news, however, is that most snakes prefer their dinner to be all but alive and kicking! A snake's idea of a hot breakfast is a freshly-killed mouse. You may be able to buy a snake that has learned to take dead meat, however, but do insist on a demonstration before you take it home!

Moody moulters

As snakes grow, they shed their old coat of scales and grow a new one. A snake that is about to moult stops feeding and goes into a sulk. If you are not sure whether your snake is sick or simply in the moulting mood, it is a good idea to ask the advice of a veterinarian.

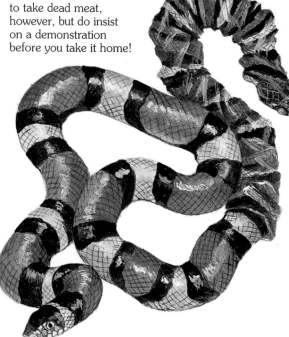

A WORM FARM

Subterranean secrets

Almost the only time we see an earthworm is when we dig in the garden. What do they do under there in the dark, damp ground? If you make a worm farm, you can find out just how they live and work, find a mate and lay eggs.

Why bother?

Earthworms are the greatest gardeners on Earth. They feed by swallowing soil and digesting the dead plant stuff in it. Although no body knows why, it is an amazing fact that soil that has been through a worm's body is extra-specially good for growing things. As well as being easy pets to keep, your worms will magically tranform useless kitchen waste into better potting soil than money can buy.

How to begin

If you want to watch your worms working, the best place to keep them is in a terrarium. Put it somewhere shady and fairly warm and half-fill it with ordinary moist garden soil.

Choosing your worms

There are many different kinds of earthworms. The best ones for a worm-farm are the short, soft, pale ones that live in places like compost heaps or among dead leaves. Leave the big, muscular ones alone - they're a lot more use to early birds looking for breakfast than they are to a worm farmer. Just pop them in. Once you have found some of the right kind of worms, all you have to do is drop them into the terrarium and wait for them to dig in.

Feeding

Now you can begin to add scraps of vegetable waste from the kitchen. Any old leaves and vegetable peelings will do, but it's best to chop them up quite small. Just drop the food on top of the soil and let the worms do the work. As time goes by, and your worms get into their stride, you can give them more and more to eat. Spray with a little water from time to time (don't drown them, though!), and just watch what they do.

What next?

If things go well, you will eventually have a terrarium full of lovely soft, dark coloured soil, just heaving with worms, but there won't be room for any more food!

What you can do now is spread a large plastic sheet on the ground and simply tip out the whole lot , worms and all, on to the sheet. You can then pick out the worms and put them in a jar while you collect the compost up to store in a plastic bag until it is needed. Put more soil into the terrarium and begin all over again.

Factory Farming

If you want your terrarium for something else, but the gardener in your family is keen for you to continue supplying magic compost, it's good to know that a worm farm works just as well - perhaps even better - in an old plastic dustbin with a perforated lid. Tell this to the gardener, hand over your worms and the benefit of your experience, and let him get on with it.

One little problem

The trouble with worms is that, if you have a keen gardener in your family, he or she might be rather upset when you want to give up worm farming and change to another pet.

HELPING WILD BIRDS

VERY INTENSIVE CARE

Leave well alone
Generally speaking, wild animals get by very well without any help from people. We are apt to forget this sometimes when, with the best of intentions, we rush to the aid of a creature that is just fine. Baby birds are the most frequent victims of our misplaced concern.

Mother knows best
As a baby bird grows up it must learn to fly and feed itself, so its mother leaves it alone until it gets hungry enough to try. A young bird, cheeping plaintively on the lawn, needs no help from us, apart from keeping the cat out of the way.

When to help
One time you can be sure a bird needs help is when you find it in your pet cat's mouth! The biggest problem here is getting the bird away gently - just one bite from those sharp teeth will turn your good deed into Puss's dinner!

Shock treatment
When you have the bird cupped safely in your hands, put in into a dark box to recover from the shock of nearly being eaten. With luck, this may be all that is necessary. In an hour or so, you will be rewarded for your small act of kindness by seeing your patient fly happily away.

When to get help
Broken wings and legs do sometimes occur, and they need proper treatment. If you find an injured bird, always consult an expert.

Nursing baby birds

You can tell a baby bird by the yellow inside its beak. Babies are usually easy to feed, and they nearly all eat insects. Just wave your hand over the bird's head and it will open its beak wide. Wave a small worm or fly, gripped in tweezers, and you can stuff the food into the bird's beak as soon as it opens. Now you're a mother bird, and you'll have to work as hard as she would. This means bringing food about every 15 minutes all day long!

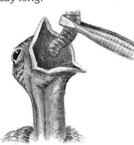

Nursing adult birds

Sometimes, an injured adult bird will open its beak like a baby. If it doesn't do this quite soon, though, you may have to begin by forcing food into its beak. This job needs a combination of firmness and gentleness, but you should soon see the patient open its beak for you when it sees the tweezers approaching.

Facing the facts

It's no use pretending that caring for injured wild birds is easy. It is very frightening for a wild creature to be handled by people, and it is also hard to give a wild bird the care and food it needs. If you succeed in nursing a hurt bird back to health, you can be very proud of your achievement. If your patient doesn't make it, don't blame yourself; it's better to have tried and lost than to have been afraid to try at all - and you may have learned something that will help you succeed next time.

CARING FOR HEDGEHOGS

Autumn orphans

Baby hedgehogs are usually born in the spring, and have all summer to grow big and fat enough to sleep through the winter. Occasionally, though, there is a second litter later in the year, and these hoglets may still be too small to hibernate when autumn comes.

Weight it and see

If you find a hoglet wandering alone in the late summer or early autumn (especially in daylight) it may need your help. The first thing to do is to weigh it. If an autumn hoglet weighs less than a pound, it stands little chance of living through the winter without assistance.

Housing hedgehogs

A good arrangement for a hoglet is a big cardboard box with a smaller one inside. Fill the small box with bedding - hay, dry dead leaves, or torn paper strips - and cut a creep-hole. If the baby is very small, it will need a hot-water bottle, too. Line the large box with several layers of newspaper. It must be really secure because hedgehogs can climb very well and are surprisingly strong.

Feeding

The best basic diet for hedgehogs is tinned cat or dog food (not fish-based). Add raw or scrambled egg, scraps of raw meat, worms and beetles if you can catch them, plus some cereal like crushed dog-biscuits, and your baby will be very well fed.

Water

Keep a shallow dish of fresh water in the big box. Don't give milk unless it is goat's milk.

Fleas and ticks

It cannot be denied that most hedgehogs have lots and lots of fleas!

These are easily destroyed by dusting a mild insecticide such as derris among the back spines and under the paper in the large box. Don't put insecticide onto a very young animal, though, or where it might go snuffling about. Sick or weak hedgehogs sometimes have ticks as well, but it is best to resist the temptation to pull them off. Wait until the tick drops off by itself, then remove it with the bedding (watch out - don't let the tick lock onto you!).

Mucking out

Hedgehogs are messy eaters, clumsy with their water, and messy in every other way, too! You must be prepared to clean out your guest's quarters completely, once or even twice a day. When the hoglet is used to you, it is a good idea to remove it to a separate box for feeding, which is when most of the mess happens.

When to let go

If your hoglet grows to over 1 lb in weight before the winter comes, it can be released on a warm dry night to find its own winter quarters. If not, then it should be over 14 lbs before it can be released on a relatively mild night - never in frost or snow - during the winter.

WILD WATER PETS

What Pets?
Just scoop out a blob of mud, a spray of weed, and a pint of water from any pond. Tip it into a wide, white bowl, let it settle, then have a good look. You are sure to find some of the animals on this page, and perhaps many more. Keep them in your aquarium to get to know them better.

Planarians
It takes concentration to spot a planarian. These little flatworms are so flat that they look like tiny elongated ink-blots gliding smoothly along. Look more closely, though, and you will see two light-coloured eyes at one end. This is the front end. Some kinds are different shades of brown, others are black. It is said that if a planarian is cut into a hundred pieces, each one will become a whole new animal.

Caddis-fly larvae

Did that bundle of little sticks move? If it did, the chances are that it's the mobile home of a caddis larva, a grub that will one day turn into a fly with hairy, moth-like wings. The case may be built of sand grains, or little rocks, leaves or many other bits and pieces. Every different type builds its case in a different way.

Other larvae

Many flying insects begin life as water creatures. Mayflies and mosquitoes, hover-flies and horseflies, craneflies and blackflies, and even some moths, grow up under water. Learn how to recognise them.

Dragonfly larvae

Dragonflies have monstrous, voracious larvae. They stalk their prey with huge, bulging eyes and snap it up with their incredible shooting jaws.

Leeches

These relatives of earthworms can be recognised by the way they move, looping along using a sucker at the front and a sucker at the back. They feed by sucking blood from fishes, snails and other creatures.

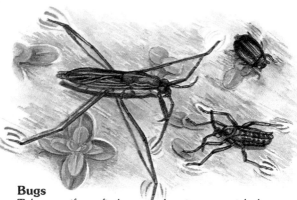

Bugs

Take care if you find a water-bug in your catch; bugs have a sharp needle to stab you!
Some water-bugs swim along on their backs, others run on the surface of the pond.

Hydra

You may find a jelly-like creature like a thin sea anemone with long arms. Use a magnifying glass to watch it move and feed.

Spiders

There are even some spiders that live in water. They manage to breathe by making a silk diving-bell and filling it with air. You may also find a bright red velvet mite, a relative of spiders.

RACK & CREVICE CREATURES

Silverfishes

When you go into the bathroom in the night, do you ever catch just a glimpse of a tiny silver tail disappearing down the drain or in to a crack in the floor?

Ancient insects

Silverfishes may have lived on Earth for 400 million years, and their staying power is matched only by their total lack of ambition.

What's for dinner?

In our homes, these tiny creatures feed on specks of food that are nearly invisible to us - little flakes of dead skin, grains of flour, anything they can find as they scurry about at night. Sometimes, they eat wallpaper paste or the glue in books, and this is practically the only time we may notice them.

Very easy pets

If you can catch a few silverfish (which is easier said than done, because they go like quicksilver), keep them in an empty chocolate box and see how fast they breed on the invisible specks that are there when we have eaten all the chocolates up! All they need is to be kept in a cool place, preferably in the dark - they won't get bored.

Firebrats

Firebrats are cousins of silverfishes that prefer hot, dry places. They choose cracks in the hearth or crannies by the boiler to set up house.

Winter visitors

In the Winter, some other creatures come into our homes for warmth. One of these is the Devil's Coach Horse, a beetle with very short wing-cases and a long jointed tail. When it is alarmed, this satin-sheened black beetle curves the end of its

tail upwards like a scorpion, and looks very alarming. But this is just an empty threat, for it cannot bite or sting you. If you find a devil's coach horse, pop it into your terrarium or put it back outside.

Earwigs

Everybody seems to hate earwigs, though they are quite harmless. In fact, they make very unusual and interesting pets. Towards the end of the summer, earwigs sometimes creep into our homes for shelter. If you can catch some then and put them into your terrarium, you may see how the female rears her babies in the spring.

Mother earwig

First, she will make a nest in the soil to lay about 50 eggs in. Then she will guard the eggs and keep them clean until they hatch. Even then her work is not finished, for her children will remain near her until they have grown big enough to look after themselves.

Now you decide

Watch an earwig family grow up, and then see whether you agree with what people say about them.